SCENE BY SCENE COMPARATIVE WORKBOOKS

FOSTER
by Claire Keegan

Cultural Context

Literary Genre

General Vision and Viewpoint

Copyright © 2015 by Amy Farrell.

All rights reserved. No part of this publication may be reproduced, distributed or transmitted in any form or by any means, including photocopying, recording, or other electronic or mechanical methods, without the prior written permission of the publisher, except in the case of brief quotations embodied in critical reviews and certain other noncommercial uses permitted by copyright law. For permission requests, write to the publisher, addressed "Attention: Permissions Coordinator," at the address below.

Scene by Scene
11 Millfield, Enniskerry
Wicklow, Ireland.
www.scenebysceneguides.com

orders@scenebyscene.ie

Foster Comparative Workbook HL16 Amy Farrell. —1st ed.
ISBN 978-1-910949-05-4

2016 Higher Level Comparative Workbook

'Foster' by Claire Keegan

The modes at Higher Level for 2016 are:

Cultural Context

This mode refers to the world of the text.

Consider social norms, beliefs, values and attitudes. Think about the roles of men and women and the power structures in this world, etc.

The General Vision and Viewpoint

This mode refers to the author's outlook or view of life and how this viewpoint is represented in the text.

Consider whether the text is bright or dark, optimistic or pessimistic, uplifting or bleak, etc.

Literary Genre

This mode refers to the way the story is told.

Consider the manner and style of narration, characterisation, setting, tension, literary techniques, etc.

About This Workbook

Our workbooks are for the Leaving Certificate Comparative Study.

Each workbook is divided into three coloured sections, one for each comparative mode. This makes it easy to identify each mode and make comparisons and contrasts between texts – simply use matching coloured sections of each of your workbooks to identify similarities and differences.

Each coloured section has two parts to it. The first part focuses on the text itself, and asks text-specific questions within a comparative mode. This helps you get familiar with the text and the aspects of the text that are covered by that mode.

The second part of each section focuses on one of the modes. In this part, you are asked more general, mode-specific questions. You then have to take what you know about the text and apply it to the mode. By doing this you will become very familiar with what each mode involves, and it will help prepare you for writing comparative answers.

Once complete, this workbook will become your set of notes, to revise and study before the exam, and to help you when preparing comparative essays for class.

We hope our workbooks help you conquer the comparative!

Best wishes,

The team at Scene by Scene

scenebysceneguides.com

Foster by Claire Keegan
Cultural Context

FOSTER - CULTURAL CONTEXT

What **time** and **place** is the story set in?

Describe the **countryside** where the story takes place.

KNOW THE TEXT

How do the characters in this story **make a living**?

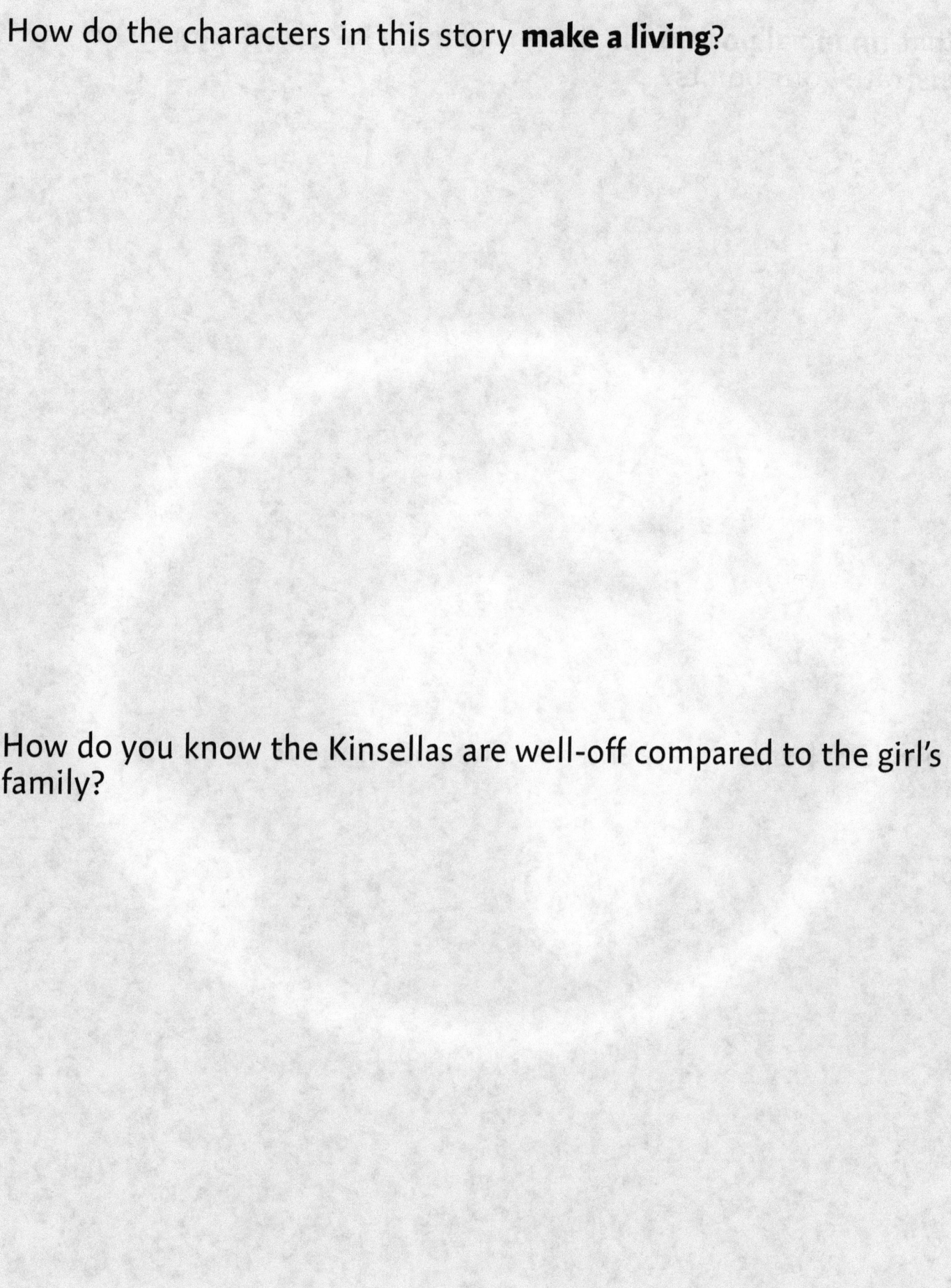

How do you know the Kinsellas are well-off compared to the girl's family?

FOSTER - CULTURAL CONTEXT

What **financial position** is the girl's family in? Use examples to illustrate your points.

How does her father spend his time and money?

KNOW THE TEXT

What is life like for the girl's mother?

How does Kinsella spend his time and money?

FOSTER - CULTURAL CONTEXT

What is life like for Edna Kinsella?

What **attitudes** are shown in the text through the character of Mildred, the neighbour who brings the girl home from the wake?

KNOW THE TEXT

What does **the wake** tell you about the **customs** of the world of the text?

What are the Kinsellas' neighbours like?

Is this a **close-knit community**?

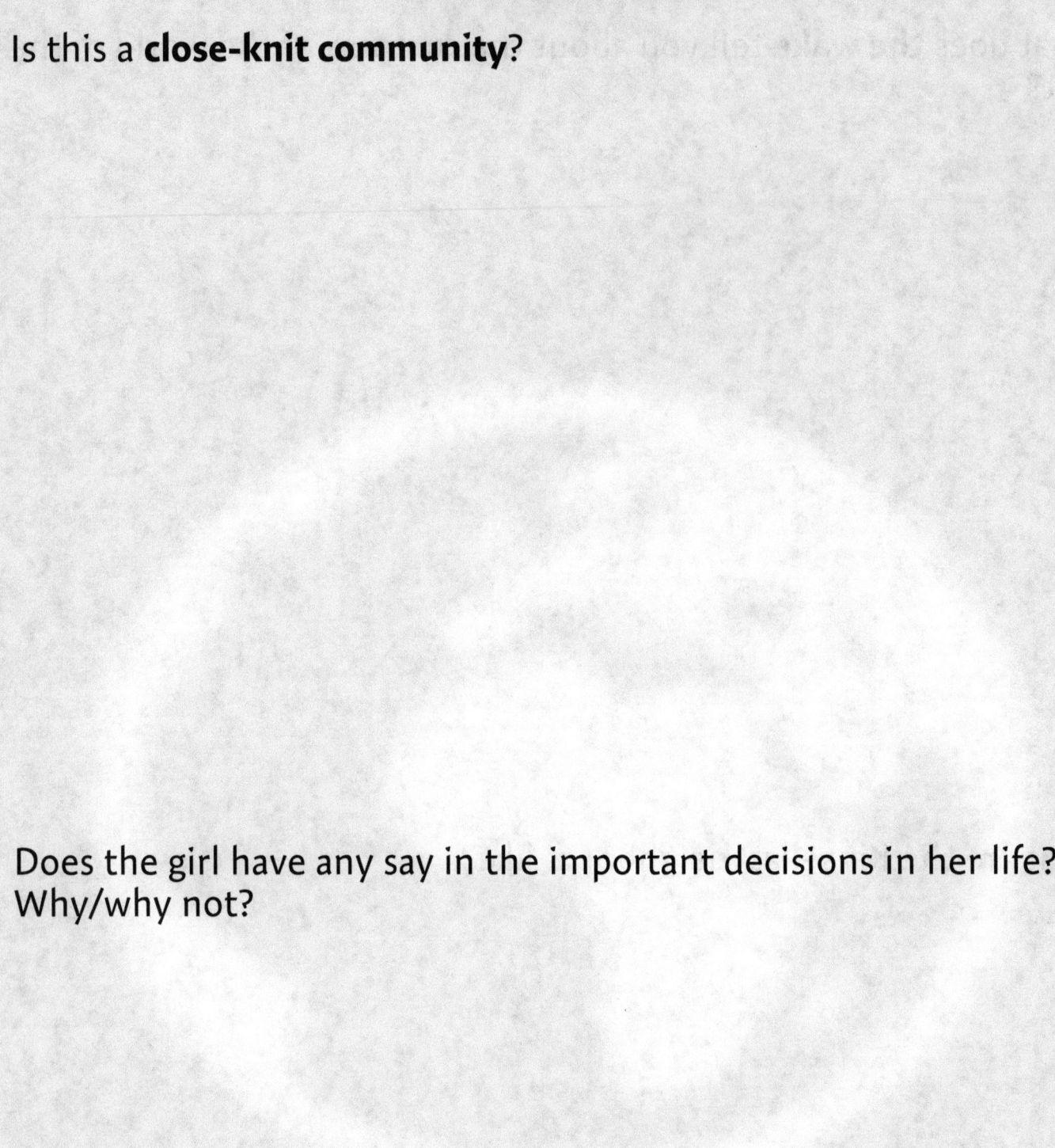

Does the girl have any say in the important decisions in her life? Why/why not?

KNOW THE TEXT

Why can't the girl choose who she wants to live with?

Are her parents very different from her foster parents? In what ways are they different? What does this tell you about the world of the text?

KNOW THE MODE

Is **religion** important in this world? What makes you say this?

Are **wealth** and **class** important in this world? What view do characters have towards **money**?

KNOW THE MODE

Do the characters in this text hold **traditional beliefs**?

FOSTER - CULTURAL CONTEXT

Is **race** important in this world?

FOSTER - CULTURAL CONTEXT

Is **race** important in this world?

KNOW THE MODE

Are characters **moral** and **upstanding** in this text?

What do people **value** in this text? (What is important to them? What motivates them to act as they do?)

KNOW THE MODE

What kind of **society** do you see in the text? (How do people treat one another? What do they believe in?)

KNOW THE MODE

Is **family** important in the world of this text?

KNOW THE MODE

How are **women** viewed and treated in this story?

FOSTER - CULTURAL CONTEXT

How are **children** viewed and treated in this story?

KNOW THE MODE

Is **friendship/love** important in this world or are characters self-centred and self-serving? (Is it a warm/loving place or a cold/unloving place?)

FOSTER - CULTURAL CONTEXT

Is there **conflict** or **violence** in this world? Where do you see it?

Is there **conflict** or **violence** in this world? Where do you see it?

KNOW THE MODE

Is this a **secure** or **dangerous** world?

KNOW THE MODE

Is this a **secure** or **dangerous** world?

In this world, do characters **conform** or make their own choices **freely?**

KNOW THE MODE

Would you like to live in the world of the text? Use examples to support the points you make.

FOSTER - CULTURAL CONTEXT

Identify the **key moments** in the novel that illustrate the Cultural Context of the text.

KNOW THE MODE

KNOW THE MODE

FOSTER - CULTURAL CONTEXT

What **similarities** do you notice in the Cultural Context of this text and your other comparative texts?

KNOW THE MODE

FOSTER - CULTURAL CONTEXT

What **differences** do you notice in the Cultural Context of this text and your other comparative texts?

KNOW THE MODE

KNOW THE MODE

Foster by Claire Keegan
Literary Genre

How is the story told? (Consider the novel format – chapter breaks, style of narration, etc.)

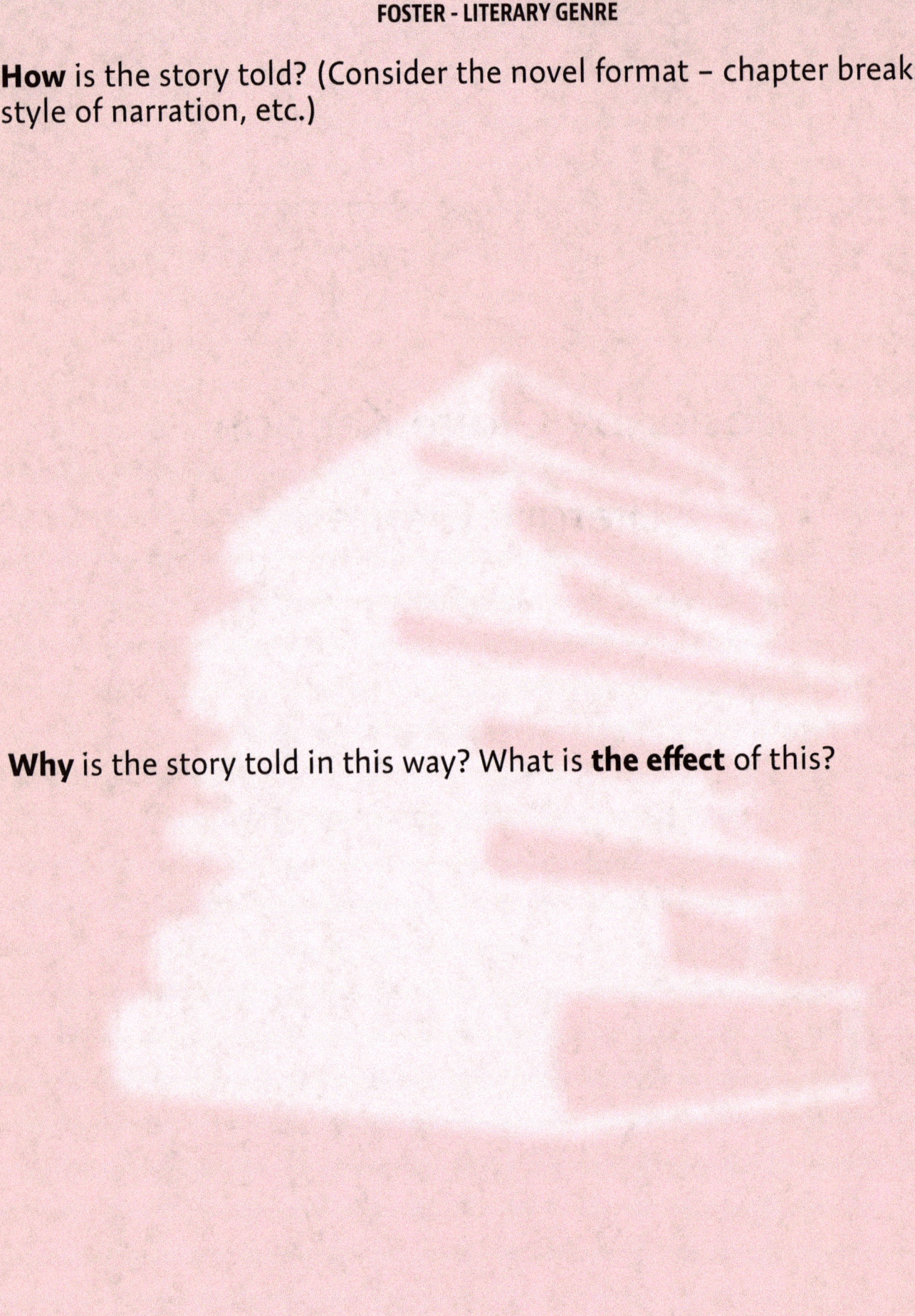

Why is the story told in this way? What is **the effect** of this?

KNOW THE TEXT

Is **the girl** a good choice of **narrator** here? Explain your reasons.

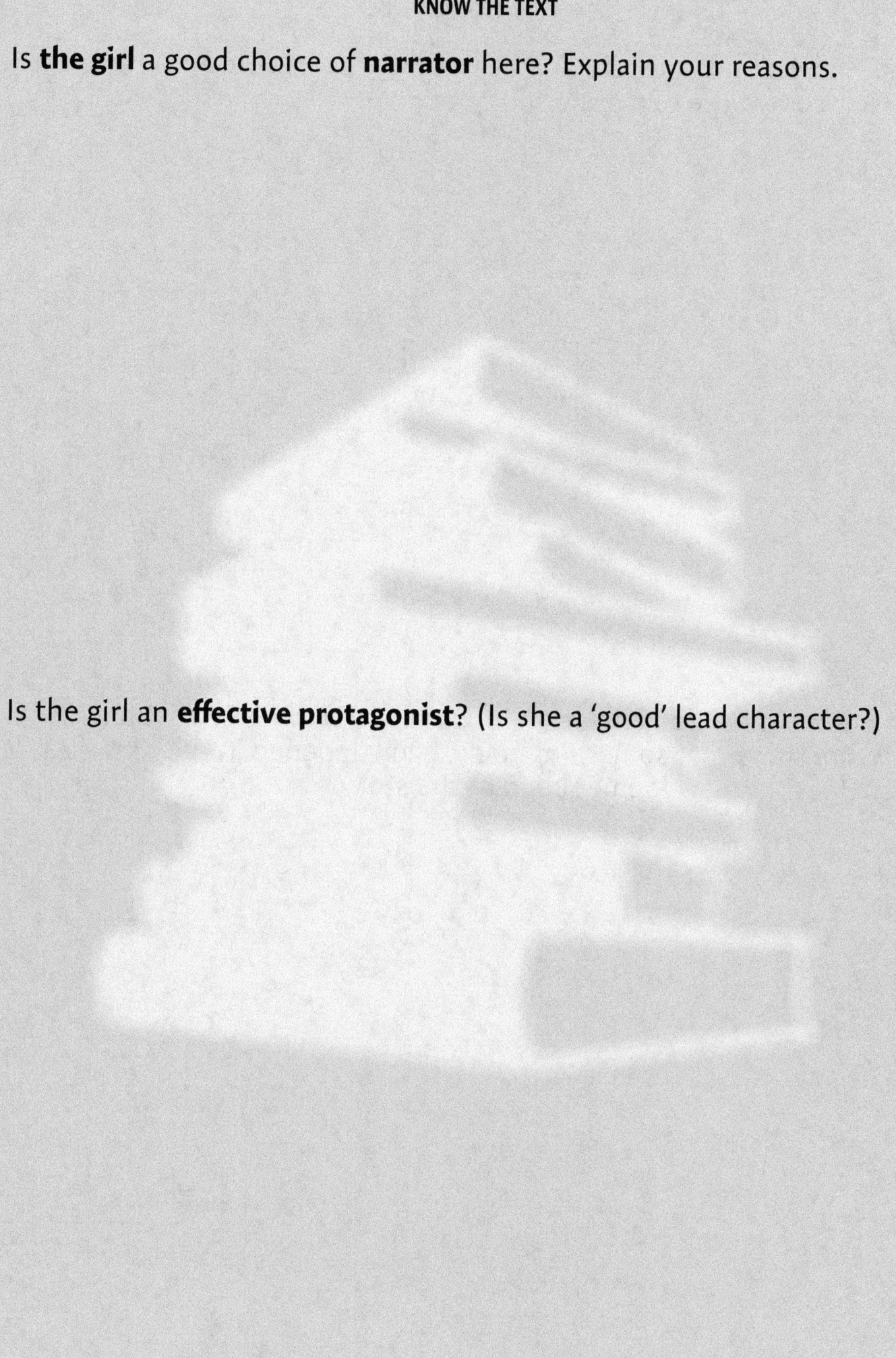

Is the girl an **effective protagonist**? (Is she a 'good' lead character?)

The **girl** doesn't fully understand everything that is going on. How does this contribute to the story?

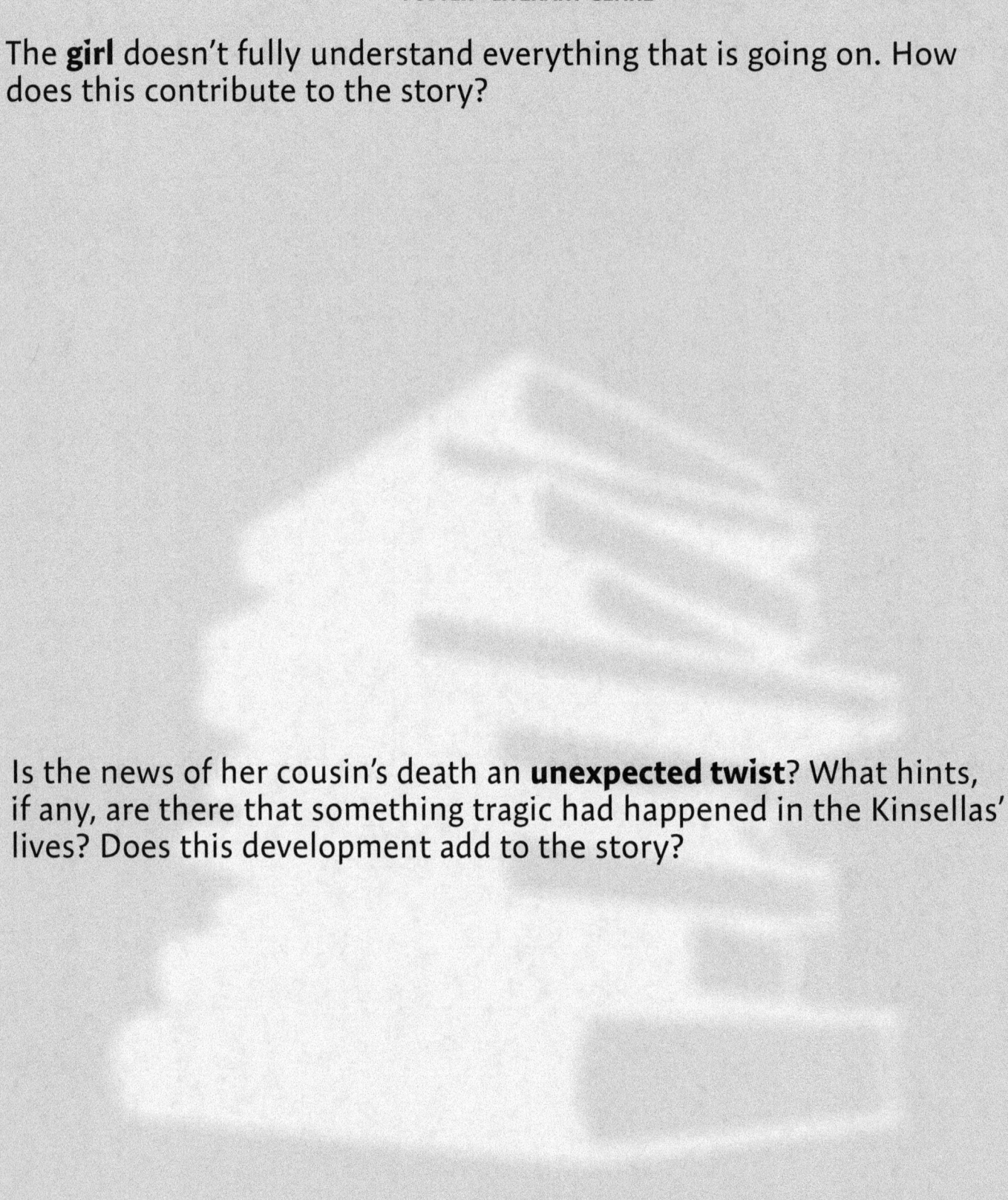

Is the news of her cousin's death an **unexpected twist**? What hints, if any, are there that something tragic had happened in the Kinsellas' lives? Does this development add to the story?

KNOW THE TEXT

How did the death of her cousin affect the course of the girl's story?

Which characters do you like? What makes them appealing?

Which characters do you dislike? What makes them unappealing?

How does the author help us to understand her characters?

KNOW THE TEXT

Is this a novel about loneliness, grief, love or something else?

What major themes can you identify?

FOSTER - LITERARY GENRE

"Foster" has been described as "beautiful, strange and moving." Do you agree with this assessment?

"Foster" has been described as "beautiful, strange and moving." Do you agree with this assessment?

KNOW THE MODE

Did **you** enjoy the **storyline** of the text? (Was it exciting/compelling/tense/emotional? Why/why not?)

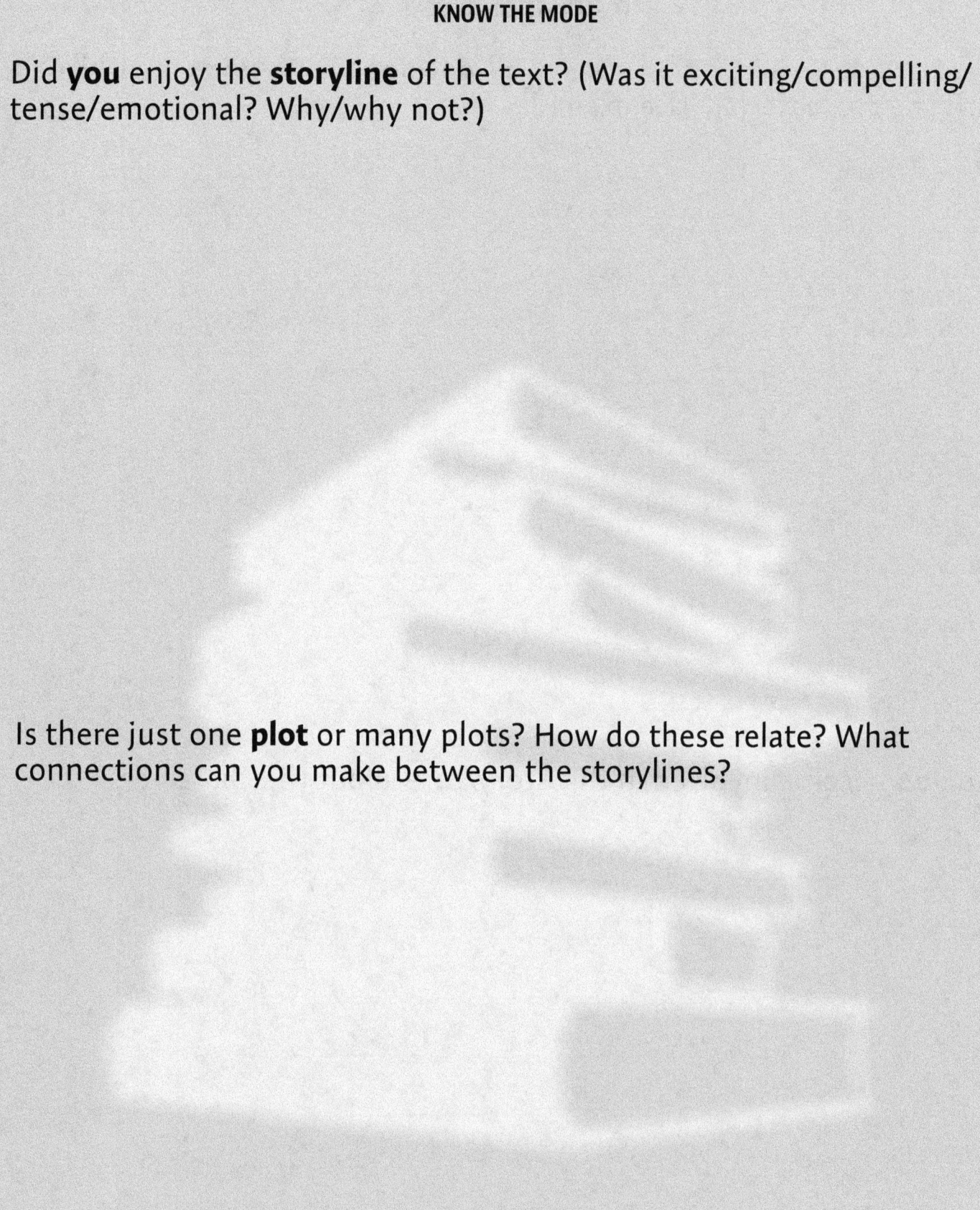

Is there just one **plot** or many plots? How do these relate? What connections can you make between the storylines?

Are **characters** vivid, realistic and well-developed? Do **you** empathise with any character(s)? Use examples.

Did **you** become involved in this story/care about the characters?

KNOW THE MODE

Who was your **favourite character**? What aspects of this character did you enjoy?

Who was your **least favourite character**? What aspects of this character did you dislike?

KNOW THE MODE

Is the story humorous or tragic, romantic or realistic? Explain.

To what **genre** does it belong? Is it Romance, Thriller, Social Realism, Saga, Historical, Fantasy, Science-fiction, Satire, etc.?

How does the author create **tension**, **suspense, high emotion** and **excitement** in the text? What literary techniques does she use to good advantage?

KNOW THE MODE

Consider the author's use of **tension** and **resolution** in the novel. What are the major **tensions/problems/conflicts** in the text? Are they **resolved** or not?

How does the author make points to her audience/force us to think/ introduce themes?

Did the author make use of any striking patterns of **imagery** or **symbols** to add to the story?

KNOW THE MODE

What is the **climax** (high point) of the story? How did you respond to it?

Comment on the **language** of the novel.

KNOW THE MODE

Comment on the **setting** of the novel.

Was anything about this novel **moving** or **emotional**? How did this emotion add to the story?

KNOW THE MODE

Did you enjoy the **ending**? What was satisfying/unsatisfying about it?

KNOW THE MODE

Did you enjoy the **ending**? What was satisfying/unsatisfying about it?

The experiences of encountering a play (performed), reading a novel and viewing a film are very different. What aspects of the **novel form** worked well in this story, in your opinion? Was **this way** of telling the story **successful** and **enjoyable**? What did **you like** about the **way this story was told**? Mention aspects of literary technique that **you** found appealing and enjoyable. (Make use of personal response – your reaction to key moments)

KNOW THE MODE

KNOW THE MODE

Identify **key moments** in the novel that illustrate Literary Genre (the way the story is told). Clearly define literary techniques in your analysis.

KNOW THE MODE

KNOW THE MODE

FOSTER - LITERARY GENRE

What **similarities** do you notice in the Literary Genre of this novel and your other comparative texts?

KNOW THE MODE

KNOW THE MODE

FOSTER - LITERARY GENRE

What **differences** do you notice in the Literary Genre of this novel and your other comparative texts?

KNOW THE MODE

KNOW THE MODE

FOSTER - LITERARY GENRE

Foster by Claire Keegan
General Vision and Viewpoint

How do you feel about the girl being sent to live with her aunt and uncle?

What sort of life does she lead at home?

KNOW THE TEXT

Is life better or worse for her with the Kinsellas?

Is the girl loved and wanted in this story?

What does learning of the death of their son, reveal to you about the Kinsellas' lives?

Why did Mildred tell the girl about this tragedy? What is your reaction to the way she broke this news?

KNOW THE TEXT

What is the atmosphere like as Kinsella and the girl go walking by the shore at night? How do you feel as you read this section?

How do the adults in the story treat one another?

Are characters in this story happy and content, or dissatisfied with life? Explain.

Did you want the girl to stay with the Kinsellas? Explain your answer.

KNOW THE TEXT

How do you feel, reading about the girl's return home?

Is the girl's future promising?

How does the closing section make you feel?

Did you anticipate a happy ending?

KNOW THE TEXT

What is Claire Keegan telling us about life in this story?

Is her outlook positive or negative, in your view?

Identify bright/hopeful/optimistic moments, or aspects of the novel.

KNOW THE MODE

Identify dark/hopeless/pessimistic moments, or aspects of the novel.

Is this text **optimistic** or **pessimistic**? Explain.

KNOW THE MODE

What **aspects of life** does the author concentrate on? Why does she do this?

FOSTER - GENERAL VISION AND VIEWPOINT

What **comments** do characters make on their **society** and the problems they're facing?

KNOW THE MODE

Are characters happy or unhappy?

FOSTER - GENERAL VISION AND VIEWPOINT

What makes characters in this story happy and fulfilled?

KNOW THE MODE

What makes characters in this story unhappy and unfulfilled?

Are **relationships** destructive or nurturing?

What do they reveal about life, as we see characters supported/thwarted in their efforts to grow/mature?

KNOW THE MODE

Are **imagery** and **language** bright or dark in the text? (Tone of the text)

What is the **mood** of this text?

KNOW THE MODE

Did you notice the use of symbolism to add to mood or atmosphere anywhere in the text?

FOSTER - GENERAL VISION AND VIEWPOINT

What does this story teach us about life?

KNOW THE MODE

What **view of life** is offered in the text?

FOSTER - GENERAL VISION AND VIEWPOINT

How do you **feel** as you read this novel?

KNOW THE MODE

How do you **feel** at the **end**?

FOSTER - GENERAL VISION AND VIEWPOINT

Are **questions** raised by the text **resolved** by the end? Are they resolved **happily** or **unhappily**?

KNOW THE MODE

Are *you* **hopeful** or **despairing** regarding the prospects for human **happiness** in this story?

On a scale of one to ten (with one being "most optimistic" and ten being "most pessimistic"), where would you place this text? Explain your choice.

FOSTER - GENERAL VISION AND VIEWPOINT

Identify the **key moments** in the novel that illustrate the General Vision and Viewpoint of the text.

KNOW THE MODE

What **similarities** do you notice in the General Vision and Viewpoint of this text and your other comparative texts?

KNOW THE MODE

What **differences** do you notice in the General Vision and Viewpoint of this text and your other comparative texts?

KNOW THE MODE

www.ingramcontent.com/pod-product-compliance
Lightning Source LLC
Chambersburg PA
CBHW050714090526
44587CB00019B/3379